A GUIDE FORAGING FOR WILD FOODS

Carolina T. Branch

Table of Contents

Introduction

Foraging, the age-old practice of gathering wild foods from the natural landscape, has experienced a resurgence in recent years. What was once a necessity for survival has now become a passion for many, driven by a desire to reconnect with nature, rediscover forgotten flavors, and embrace a more sustainable lifestyle. In this introductory section, we delve into the various aspects that make foraging a rewarding and enriching pursuit, while also highlighting the importance of ethics, safety, proper tools, and understanding the delicate balance of ecosystems.

a. Why Forage?

At its core, foraging is about forging a deeper connection with the natural world. It offers a way to engage with the environment on a more intimate level, fostering a sense of wonder and appreciation for the bounty that nature provides. Beyond its inherent beauty, foraging holds practical benefits as well. Wild foods are often nutrient-rich, diverse, and free from the pesticides and additives commonly found in commercially grown produce. By foraging, individuals can supplement their diets with fresh, wholesome ingredients while reducing their ecological footprint.

Furthermore, foraging can be a gateway to cultural heritage and culinary exploration. Many traditional cuisines around the world incorporate wild ingredients, celebrating the unique flavors and textures they offer. By learning to identify and harvest wild edibles, foragers can tap into this rich culinary heritage, discovering new ways to prepare and enjoy food.

b. Ethics and Safety Considerations

While foraging can be a deeply rewarding activity, it is not without its risks and responsibilities. Ethical considerations are paramount when gathering wild foods, as overharvesting or careless foraging practices can have detrimental effects on ecosystems and local wildlife populations. Foragers must tread lightly, following principles of sustainability and conservation to ensure that they leave minimal impact on the environment.

Safety is another critical aspect of foraging, as misidentification of plants or mushrooms can lead to serious illness or even death. Foragers must educate themselves thoroughly on the species they intend to harvest, learning to distinguish between edible and poisonous varieties. Additionally, foragers should be aware of potential environmental hazards such as contaminated water sources or polluted landscapes, taking appropriate precautions to safeguard their health and well-being.

c. Getting Started: Essential Tools and Gear

Before setting out on a foraging expedition, it is essential to gather the proper tools and gear. While the specific equipment may vary depending on the environment and the types of wild foods being sought, there are some essential items that every forager should have:

- A field guide or smartphone app for plant and mushroom identification
- Sturdy footwear and appropriate clothing for the terrain and weather conditions
- Containers for collecting and transporting harvested foods, such as baskets or mesh bags
- Gardening gloves or hand tools for safe handling of thorny or prickly plants
- A water bottle and snacks to stay hydrated and energized during foraging outings

By equipping themselves with the right gear, foragers can enhance their safety and efficiency in the field, making the experience more enjoyable and rewarding.

d. Understanding Seasonality and Ecosystems

Seasonality plays a crucial role in foraging, as the availability of wild foods can vary greatly throughout the year. By understanding the natural cycles of plant growth and reproduction, foragers can better predict when certain species will be ripe for harvest. Additionally, foragers must be attuned to the specific ecosystems in which they are foraging, as different plants and fungi thrive in different habitats.

Ecosystem awareness is essential for practicing ethical foraging, as it allows foragers to recognize the interconnectedness of all living beings and the delicate balance that must be maintained for ecosystems to flourish. By respecting the natural rhythms of the environment and harvesting with care and consideration, foragers can ensure the long-term sustainability of wild food sources for future generations.

In conclusion, foraging is not just about gathering food; it is a holistic experience that encompasses a deep appreciation for nature, a commitment to ethical principles, and a sense of stewardship for the land. By embracing the values of ethics, safety, proper tools, and ecosystem awareness, foragers can embark on a journey of discovery and connection that nourishes both body and soul.

CHAPTER ONE

Identifying Wild Edibles

Identification is the cornerstone of successful foraging. In this chapter, we delve into the essential techniques and knowledge needed to confidently identify edible plants and fungi in the wild. From understanding key features to recognizing common species and avoiding potentially harmful look-alikes, mastering the art of identification is crucial for safe and enjoyable foraging experiences.

1. Key Features for Identification

Identifying wild edibles requires keen observation and attention to detail. While there is no one-size-fits-all approach to identification, certain key features can help foragers narrow down their options and make accurate determinations. These features include:

- Leaf shape, arrangement, and texture: Leaves can vary widely in size, shape, and texture, providing valuable clues to a plant's identity. Pay close attention to leaf margins, venation patterns, and overall growth habits.
- Flower structure and color: Flowers are often the most distinctive feature of a plant, offering important clues to its identity. Note the size, shape, color, and arrangement of petals, as well

as the presence of any distinctive markings or structures.

- Fruit and seed characteristics: Fruits and seeds can vary greatly among different plant species, providing valuable information for identification. Pay attention to fruit size, shape, color, and texture, as well as any unique features such as spines or hairs.
- Growth habitat and ecological niche: Many plants have specific habitat preferences and ecological requirements, which can help narrow down their identity. Pay attention to the types of ecosystems in which a plant is found, as well as its preferred soil type, moisture levels, and sun exposure.

By honing their observational skills and familiarizing themselves with these key features, foragers can become more adept at identifying wild edibles with confidence.

2. Common Edible Plants and Fungi

There is a wealth of edible plants and fungi waiting to be discovered in the wild. From familiar favorites like dandelions and blackberries to lesser-known treasures like wild ramps and hen-of-the-woods mushrooms, the possibilities for culinary exploration are endless. In this section, we highlight some of the most commonly foraged edible species, including:

- Wild greens and herbs: Dandelion greens, lamb's quarters, and purslane are just a few examples of nutritious greens that can be found growing wild in fields, meadows, and forest edges.
- Berries and fruits: From sweet strawberries and blueberries to tart blackberries and elderberries, wild fruits are a delicious and abundant source of seasonal bounty.
- Mushrooms and fungi: While mushroom foraging requires extra caution and expertise, many delicious and highly prized culinary mushrooms can be found in the wild, including chanterelles, morels, and porcini.

By familiarizing themselves with these common edible species and their preferred habitats, foragers can increase their chances of success in the field and enjoy a diverse array of wild foods throughout the seasons.

3. Poisonous Look-Alikes: How to Avoid Them

One of the biggest challenges for foragers is distinguishing between edible species and their poisonous look-alikes. Many plants and fungi have toxic counterparts that closely resemble their edible counterparts, making accurate identification essential for safety. Some common examples of poisonous look-alikes include:

- Deadly nightshade (Atropa belladonna) vs. blackberries (Rubus spp.): Both plants produce small, dark berries, but deadly nightshade berries are highly toxic if ingested.
- False morels (Gyromitra spp.) vs. true morels (Morchella spp.): While true morels are prized for their delicious flavor, false morels contain a potentially deadly toxin and should be avoided.
- Poison hemlock (Conium maculatum) vs. wild carrots (Daucus carota): Both plants belong to the Apiaceae family and have similar foliage, but poison hemlock is highly toxic if ingested.

To avoid dangerous mistakes, foragers should always err on the side of caution and consult multiple reputable sources for identification confirmation. When in doubt, it is best to leave a plant or fungus untouched rather than risk potential harm.

Tips for Successful Identification

- Start with the basics: Begin by learning to identify a few common and easily recognizable species before branching out to more challenging ones.
- Use multiple sources: Consult field guides, online resources, and local experts to cross-reference information and confirm identifications.

- Pay attention to detail: Take note of subtle differences in leaf shape, flower structure, and growth habits that can help distinguish between similar species.
- Practice caution: When in doubt, refrain from harvesting and consuming wild foods until you are confident in your identification skills.

By following these tips and guidelines, foragers can enhance their ability to accurately identify edible plants and fungi in the wild, ensuring a safe and rewarding foraging experience.

CHAPTER TWO

Harvesting Techniques

Harvesting wild foods is a delicate balance between gathering what we need and ensuring the continued health and vitality of natural ecosystems. In this chapter, we explore the principles of sustainable harvesting, proper techniques for harvesting various types of wild foods, methods for preserving harvested foods, and the importance of leaving no trace in the wild.

1. Sustainable Harvesting Practices

Sustainability lies at the heart of responsible foraging. To ensure the long-term viability of wild food sources, foragers must adopt practices that minimize their impact on natural ecosystems and promote ecological resilience. Some key principles of sustainable harvesting include:

- Harvesting selectively: Instead of depleting entire populations of wild plants or fungi, foragers should aim to harvest only a small portion of the available resources, leaving the majority to reproduce and replenish.

- Practicing rotation: By rotating harvesting locations and allowing time for regrowth between harvests, foragers can prevent overexploitation of specific areas and promote biodiversity.
- Respecting seasonal cycles: Many wild plants and fungi have specific growing seasons during which they are most abundant and resilient. Foragers should time their harvests to coincide with these natural rhythms, avoiding harvesting during sensitive periods such as flowering or seed production.
- Being mindful of sensitive habitats: Certain ecosystems, such as wetlands, fragile alpine environments, and rare plant communities, are particularly vulnerable to human disturbance. Foragers should exercise caution when harvesting in these areas, minimizing their impact and adhering to any local regulations or guidelines.

By incorporating these sustainable harvesting practices into their foraging routines, individuals can enjoy the bounty of wild foods while preserving the integrity and resilience of natural ecosystems for future generations.

2. Proper Techniques for Picking, Digging, and Cutting

Harvesting wild foods requires finesse and care to minimize damage to plants, fungi, and their surrounding habitats. Depending on the type of food being harvested, different techniques may be required:

- **Picking:** When harvesting fruits, berries, or tender greens, gently grasp the stem or fruiting body and pluck it from the plant with a slight twisting motion to avoid damaging the surrounding foliage.
- **Digging:** For root vegetables or tuberous plants, use a small trowel or digging tool to carefully excavate the soil around the base of the plant, taking care not to disturb neighboring plants or soil structure.
- **Cutting:** When harvesting mushrooms or woody herbs, use a sharp knife or scissors to make clean, precise cuts at the base of the stem or branch, leaving behind the roots or base intact to facilitate regrowth.

Regardless of the harvesting technique used, foragers should always be mindful of their impact on the surrounding ecosystem and strive to minimize disturbance to plant and animal life.

3. Methods for Preserving Wild Foods

Preserving harvested foods allows foragers to enjoy the bounty of the wild long after the harvest season has passed. There are several methods for preserving wild foods, including:

- **Drying:** Many wild herbs, mushrooms, and fruits can be dried and stored for later use. Simply spread the harvested foods in a single layer on a drying rack or mesh screen in a well-ventilated area until they are completely dry, then store them in airtight containers.
- **Freezing:** Certain wild foods, such as berries and mushrooms, can be frozen for long-term storage. Wash and prepare the foods as desired, then spread them out on a baking sheet in a single layer and freeze until solid before transferring them to freezer-safe containers.
- **Canning:** Canning is an excellent way to preserve wild foods such as jams, pickles, and sauces. Follow approved canning recipes and techniques to ensure safe preservation and storage of canned goods.
- **Fermenting:** Fermentation is a traditional method of preserving foods that not only extends their shelf life but also enhances their flavor and nutritional value. Wild vegetables, fruits, and even mushrooms can be fermented into delicious and probiotic-rich foods such as sauerkraut, kimchi, and pickles.

By mastering these preservation techniques, foragers can enjoy the flavors of the wild year-round and reduce waste by making the most of their harvests.

Leave No Trace: Tread Lightly Principles

In addition to sustainable harvesting practices, foragers should also adhere to the principles of Leave No Trace (LNT) and Tread Lightly when exploring wild spaces. These principles emphasize minimizing human impact on the environment and preserving the natural beauty and integrity of outdoor areas. Some key LNT principles for foragers include:

- **Plan ahead and prepare:** Research local regulations and guidelines before heading out on a foraging expedition, and make sure to obtain any necessary permits or permissions.
- **Dispose of waste properly:** Pack out all trash and leftover materials, including food scraps, packaging, and biodegradable waste. Leave the foraging area cleaner than you found it.
- **Respect wildlife:** Minimize disturbances to wildlife by observing from a distance and avoiding activities that could disrupt their natural behaviors or habitats.
- **Be considerate of other visitors:** Share the trails and foraging areas with courtesy and respect for other outdoor enthusiasts,

maintaining a low profile and minimizing noise and visual impacts.

By following these principles and practicing responsible stewardship of the land, foragers can enjoy the beauty and bounty of the wild while ensuring that future generations can do the same.

CHAPTER THREE

Wild Food Preparation

In this chapter, we delve into the art and science of preparing wild foods for consumption. From cleaning and processing harvested edibles to exploring various cooking methods and recipes, we discover how to transform nature's bounty into delicious and nutritious meals. Additionally, we explore the rich tapestry of traditional and cultural uses of wild foods, shedding light on the diverse culinary traditions that have evolved around the world.

1. Cleaning and Processing Wild Edibles

Before wild foods can be enjoyed, they must undergo careful cleaning and processing to remove any dirt, debris, or unwanted contaminants. Depending on the type of food being prepared, different cleaning methods may be required:

- **Washing:** Many wild greens, fruits, and vegetables can be washed thoroughly under running water to remove surface dirt and bacteria. Use a gentle scrub brush or cloth to clean hard-to-reach areas, and pat dry with a clean towel.

- **Soaking:** Some wild foods, such as mushrooms and root vegetables, benefit from soaking in cold water to remove excess dirt and grit. Allow the foods to soak for a few minutes, then rinse and pat dry before use.
- **Trimming**: Trim away any bruised, damaged, or spoiled areas of wild foods before cooking or preserving them. Use a sharp knife or kitchen shears to remove any undesirable parts, taking care to preserve as much of the edible portion as possible.

By taking the time to clean and process wild foods properly, foragers can ensure that they are safe and enjoyable to eat, free from any unwanted contaminants or impurities.

2. Cooking Methods and Recipes

Wild foods can be prepared using a wide range of cooking methods, from simple techniques such as sautéing and grilling to more elaborate methods such as braising and roasting. Experimentation is key to discovering the best ways to highlight the flavors and textures of wild ingredients. Some popular cooking methods for wild foods include:

- **Sautéing:** Quickly cooking wild greens, mushrooms, or vegetables in a hot skillet with a bit of oil or butter until tender and lightly browned.

- **Grilling:** Grilling wild meats, fish, or vegetables over an open flame or on a hot grill until charred and smoky, imparting a delicious flavor to the foods.
- **Braising:** Slow-cooking tough or fibrous wild meats or root vegetables in a flavorful liquid such as broth or wine until tender and succulent.
- **Roasting:** Roasting wild fruits, nuts, or vegetables in the oven until caramelized and golden brown, enhancing their natural sweetness and richness.

In addition to cooking methods, there are countless recipes that showcase the versatility and culinary potential of wild foods. From wild mushroom risotto to nettle soup to venison stew, the possibilities are limited only by one's imagination and creativity.

3. Incorporating Wild Ingredients into Everyday Meals

While foraging may conjure images of rustic, outdoor cooking, wild ingredients can also be incorporated into everyday meals to add flavor, nutrition, and excitement to the dining experience. From salads and stir-fries to soups and sandwiches, wild foods can elevate ordinary dishes to extraordinary heights.

Some tips for incorporating wild ingredients into everyday meals include:

- **Start simple**: Begin by adding small amounts of wild ingredients to familiar recipes, gradually increasing the quantity as you become more comfortable with their flavors and textures.
- **Be creative:** Don't be afraid to experiment with new flavor combinations and cooking techniques to showcase the unique qualities of wild ingredients.
- **Think beyond the plate:** Wild foods can also be used to infuse oils, vinegars, and spirits, adding depth and complexity to dressings, marinades, and cocktails.

By incorporating wild ingredients into everyday meals, foragers can enjoy the flavors of the wild year-round, infusing their cooking with a sense of adventure and connection to the natural world.

Traditional and Cultural Uses of Wild Foods

Throughout history, cultures around the world have relied on wild foods for sustenance, flavor, and cultural significance. From Native American tribes to Indigenous communities in Africa, Asia, and beyond, wild foods have played a central role in traditional diets and culinary practices. Some examples of traditional and cultural uses of wild foods include:

- **Medicinal uses:** Many wild plants and fungi have been used for centuries in traditional medicine to treat a wide range of ailments, from digestive issues to respiratory conditions to skin ailments.
- **Ceremonial uses**: Wild foods are often incorporated into religious and ceremonial rituals as offerings to spirits or deities, symbolizing gratitude, abundance, and connection to the land.
- **Seasonal celebrations**: Wild foods are frequently featured in seasonal festivals and celebrations, marking important milestones in the agricultural calendar and honoring the cycles of nature.

By exploring the traditional and cultural uses of wild foods, foragers can gain a deeper appreciation for the cultural heritage and culinary diversity that surrounds them, enriching their culinary experiences and deepening their connection to the land.

CHAPTER FOUR

Advanced Foraging Skills

In this chapter, we delve into the realm of advanced foraging, exploring techniques and strategies for navigating challenging terrain, expanding your foraging repertoire, and discovering the world of foraged beverages and medicinal plants. These advanced skills open up new avenues for exploration and deepen your connection to the natural world.

1. Navigating More Challenging Terrain

As your foraging skills progress, you may find yourself drawn to more remote and challenging environments in search of rare and elusive wild foods. Navigating these rugged landscapes requires a combination of physical stamina, wilderness knowledge, and navigational skills. Some tips for navigating more challenging terrain include:

- **Wilderness survival skills:** Brush up on essential wilderness survival skills such as map reading, orienteering, and shelter building to ensure your safety and well-being in remote environments.

- **Safety precautions**: Always inform someone of your intended route and expected return time before venturing into challenging terrain, and carry essential safety gear such as a first aid kit, emergency shelter, and communication device.
- **Respect for nature:** Practice Leave No Trace principles and tread lightly on the land, minimizing your impact on fragile ecosystems and respecting the natural rhythms of the wilderness.

2. Expanding Your Foraging Repertoire

As you become more proficient in identifying and harvesting wild foods, you may wish to expand your foraging repertoire to include a wider variety of plant and fungal species. This can involve exploring new habitats, learning about lesser-known edible species, and experimenting with unconventional ingredients. Some ways to expand your foraging repertoire include:

- **Research and experimentation:** Take the time to research local flora and fauna, and experiment with different species to discover their unique flavors, textures, and culinary uses.
- **Networking and collaboration:** Connect with other foragers, herbalists, and wild food

enthusiasts to share knowledge, exchange tips, and collaborate on foraging outings and projects.

- **Continued learning:** Attend workshops, classes, and guided foraging tours to deepen your understanding of wild foods and learn from experienced instructors.

By continuously expanding your foraging repertoire, you can enrich your culinary experiences and cultivate a deeper appreciation for the diversity of the natural world.

3. Diving into Foraged Beverages: Teas, Infusions, and Brews

Foraging is not limited to edible foods; the wild also offers an abundance of ingredients for crafting delicious and nourishing beverages. From herbal teas and floral infusions to fermented brews and wildcrafted cocktails, the possibilities for foraged beverages are endless. Some popular foraged beverages include:

- **Herbal teas:** Harvest aromatic herbs such as mint, chamomile, and lemon balm to brew soothing and aromatic herbal teas that promote relaxation and well-being.
- **Infusions**: Experiment with infusing wild fruits, berries, and flowers into water, vinegar,

or alcohol to create flavorful and refreshing infusions for sipping on hot summer days.

- **Fermented brews**: Explore the world of wild fermentation by fermenting fruits, berries, and botanicals into delicious and probiotic-rich beverages such as kombucha, mead, and wild yeast sodas.

Foraging for Medicinal Plants

In addition to their culinary uses, many wild plants and fungi have long been valued for their medicinal properties. Foraging for medicinal plants allows you to tap into the healing power of nature and cultivate a deeper connection to traditional herbal medicine. Some common medicinal plants that can be foraged include:

- **Elderberry (Sambucus nigra):** Known for its immune-boosting properties, elderberry is used to make syrups, tinctures, and teas for treating colds, flu, and respiratory infections.
- **Plantain (Plantago spp.):** A common weed with anti-inflammatory and wound-healing properties, plantain leaves can be used to make poultices, salves, and herbal infusions for treating cuts, scrapes, and insect bites.
- **Reishi mushroom (Ganoderma lucidum):** Revered for its adaptogenic and immune-modulating effects, reishi mushroom

is used to make decoctions, tinctures, and teas for promoting overall health and vitality.

By learning to identify and responsibly harvest medicinal plants, you can harness the healing power of nature and incorporate herbal remedies into your wellness routine.

By honing your skills in navigating challenging terrain, expanding your foraging repertoire, exploring foraged beverages, and foraging for medicinal plants, you can take your foraging adventures to the next level and deepen your connection to the natural world.

CHAPTER FIVE

Foraging for Specific Environments

Foraging opportunities vary significantly across different environments, each offering unique challenges and rewards. In this chapter, we explore the art of foraging in diverse settings, from the dense cover of woodlands and forests to the dynamic ecosystems of coastal regions, the unexpected bounty of urban landscapes, and the rarified air of high altitudes. Each environment requires specific knowledge and techniques to successfully harvest its wild foods.

1. Woodlands and Forests

Woodlands and forests are rich, biodiverse environments that provide an abundance of edible plants, mushrooms, and other wild foods. To successfully forage in these settings, foragers must develop a keen eye for identifying species that thrive in the dappled light and diverse microhabitats of wooded areas.

- **Key Edibles**: Common woodland edibles include various berries (such as blackberries and raspberries), nuts (like acorns and chestnuts), edible greens (such as wild garlic and sorrel), and mushrooms (including chanterelles, morels, and porcini).

- **Foraging Tips**: Pay attention to the forest floor, fallen logs, and shaded areas where mushrooms often grow. Learn to identify trees, as many wild edibles have symbiotic relationships with specific tree species. Be aware of seasonal changes and time your foraging to coincide with the peak availability of different species.
- **Safety Considerations**: Always double-check your mushroom identifications with multiple sources, as many edible mushrooms have toxic look-alikes. Be mindful of wildlife, and avoid disturbing nests or dens.

2. Coastal Regions

Coastal regions offer a diverse array of foraging opportunities, from tidal pools teeming with marine life to salt-tolerant plants and seaweeds along the shore. Foraging in these environments requires knowledge of tides, marine biology, and coastal plant species.

- **Key Edibles**: Edibles in coastal regions include seaweeds (such as kelp and nori), shellfish (like clams, mussels, and oysters), coastal plants (such as samphire and sea rocket), and fish.

- **Foraging Tips**: Check local regulations and guidelines, as many coastal areas have specific rules regarding the harvesting of marine life. Use a tide chart to plan your foraging trips around low tide when tidal pools and mudflats are exposed. Learn to identify safe and sustainable harvesting practices for shellfish to avoid overharvesting and pollution.
- **Safety Considerations**: Be aware of potential hazards such as slippery rocks, strong currents, and sharp shells. Only harvest shellfish from clean, unpolluted waters to avoid contamination and foodborne illnesses.

3. Urban Foraging

Urban foraging involves finding edible plants and other wild foods in city and suburban environments. While it may seem unlikely, many edible species thrive in urban areas, offering a surprising bounty for the observant forager.

- **Key Edibles**: Common urban edibles include fruit trees (such as apple, pear, and cherry trees), edible weeds (like dandelions, purslane, and chickweed), and overlooked garden plants (such as nasturtiums and lamb's quarters).

- **Foraging Tips**: Focus on parks, community gardens, and neglected green spaces where edible plants are likely to be found. Always seek permission before foraging on private property. Use urban foraging as an opportunity to educate others about the edible potential of their surroundings.
- **Safety Considerations**: Avoid areas that may be contaminated by pollutants, such as roadsides, industrial sites, or areas treated with pesticides. Wash all foraged items thoroughly before consuming them.

High Altitude Foraging

High altitude environments, such as mountain regions, present unique foraging opportunities and challenges. The thinner air, cooler temperatures, and shorter growing seasons at high elevations shape the types of edible plants and fungi that can be found.

- **Key Edibles**: Edibles in high altitude regions include berries (such as wild blueberries and huckleberries), alpine herbs (like yarrow and wild thyme), and edible roots (such as osha and wild onions).
- **Foraging Tips**: Pay attention to the unique microclimates and ecological niches within high altitude environments. Timing is crucial, as the growing season is short. Look for

sheltered areas and south-facing slopes where plants may be more abundant.

- **Safety Considerations**: Be prepared for sudden weather changes and challenging terrain. Altitude can affect physical performance, so acclimatize slowly and stay hydrated. Watch out for protected or endangered species that may be present in high altitude ecosystems.

By understanding the specific characteristics and challenges of these diverse environments, foragers can expand their skills and knowledge, opening up new avenues for discovering and enjoying wild foods. Whether exploring dense forests, coastal shores, urban landscapes, or high mountain meadows, each environment offers unique rewards and experiences for the adventurous forager.

CHAPTER SIX

Foraging with a Purpose

Foraging goes beyond simply gathering food; it is a multifaceted practice that can serve various meaningful purposes. In this chapter, we explore the purposeful aspects of foraging, including sourcing medicinal plants, enhancing food security and self-sufficiency, fostering a deep connection with nature, and engaging in mindfulness. Each purpose enriches the foraging experience and contributes to a holistic approach to living sustainably and mindfully.

1. Foraging for Medicinal Plants

Foraging for medicinal plants taps into ancient traditions of herbal medicine, offering natural remedies for a range of ailments. By learning to identify, harvest, and prepare medicinal plants, foragers can create their own natural pharmacy.

- **Common Medicinal Plants**:
  - **Echinacea (Echinacea spp.)**: Boosts the immune system and helps fight colds and infections.

- **Chamomile (Matricaria chamomilla)**: Used for its calming effects and to aid digestion.
  - St. John's Wort (Hypericum perforatum): Known for its antidepressant properties.
  - **Yarrow (Achillea millefolium)**: Utilized for wound healing and reducing inflammation.
- **Harvesting Tips**:
  - Harvest plants when they are most potent, usually during the flowering stage.
  - Use sustainable practices to ensure plant populations are not depleted.
  - Dry herbs properly to preserve their medicinal properties.
- **Preparation Methods**:
  - **Teas and Infusions**: Simple and effective for extracting beneficial compounds.
  - **Tinctures**: Alcohol-based extracts that concentrate the plant's active ingredients.
  - **Salves and Balms**: Topical applications for skin ailments and wounds.

By integrating medicinal plant foraging into your routine, you can support your health naturally while maintaining a deep connection with the healing power of plants.

2. Foraging for Food Security and Self-Sufficiency

Foraging contributes to food security and self-sufficiency by providing a reliable source of nutritious and free food. It reduces dependency on commercial food systems and enhances resilience.

- **Benefits**:
    - Access to fresh, nutritious, and diverse foods.
    - Reduced grocery bills and less reliance on supermarkets.
    - Increased food sovereignty and independence from global supply chains.
- **Key Edibles for Food Security**:
    - **Nut trees**: Such as acorns and chestnuts, which provide essential fats and proteins.
    - **Wild greens**: Such as dandelion, nettle, and lamb's quarters, rich in vitamins and minerals.
    - **Fruits and berries**: Including blackberries, elderberries, and wild apples for antioxidants and natural sugars.
- **Practical Tips**:
    - Learn to preserve and store foraged foods through drying, fermenting, and canning.

- o Create a seasonal calendar to track the availability of different wild foods.
  - o Share knowledge and resources with your community to build a collective food security network.

Foraging empowers individuals and communities by enhancing their ability to secure nutritious food locally and sustainably.

3. Foraging as a Form of Connection with Nature

Foraging fosters a deep, reciprocal relationship with nature. It encourages awareness, appreciation, and stewardship of the environment.

- **Benefits**:
  - o Increased knowledge and appreciation of local ecosystems.
  - o A deeper understanding of natural cycles and seasonal changes.
  - o A sense of responsibility and stewardship towards the environment.
- **Practices to Enhance Connection**:
  - o Spend time observing and learning about different plant and animal species in your foraging area.
  - o Participate in local conservation efforts and habitat restoration projects.

- o Practice gratitude and mindfulness while foraging, recognizing the gifts of the natural world.

Foraging nurtures a profound sense of belonging and responsibility towards the earth, promoting sustainable and respectful interactions with nature.

4. Foraging as a Mindfulness Practice

Foraging can be a deeply meditative and mindful practice, fostering a state of presence and awareness.

- **Mindfulness Benefits**:
  - o Reduces stress and anxiety by fostering a sense of calm and focus.
  - o Enhances sensory awareness and connection to the present moment.
  - o Encourages a slower, more intentional pace of life.
- **Mindful Foraging Practices**:
  - o Engage all your senses while foraging: listen to the sounds of nature, observe the colors and shapes of plants, and feel the textures of leaves and soil.
  - o Practice mindful walking, paying attention to each step and the sensations in your body.
  - o Reflect on your experiences and feelings during foraging, perhaps keeping a

journal to record your thoughts and observations.

- **Integration into Daily Life**:
  - Use foraging as a time to disconnect from technology and reconnect with yourself and the natural world.
  - Share your mindful foraging experiences with others, creating a community of practice and support.

By approaching foraging as a mindfulness practice, you can enhance your well-being, deepen your connection to nature, and cultivate a greater sense of peace and presence in your daily life.

Foraging with a purpose enriches the practice, transforming it from a simple act of gathering food into a meaningful and multifaceted engagement with the natural world. Whether for medicinal use, food security, connection with nature, or mindfulness, purposeful foraging offers profound benefits and opportunities for growth and discovery.